ARE YOU READY FOR THAT JOB INTERVIEW

TRACIE-ANN RICHARDS

Copyright © 2022 Tracie-Ann Joy Richards All Rights Reserved

ISBN-: 978-0-578-26529-2

No part of this publication may be reproduced, stored, or transmitted in any form or by any means, electronic, mechanical, photocopying, recording, scanning, or otherwise, except as permitted under Section 107 or 108 of the 1976 United States Copyright Act, without the prior written permission of the author. Requests to the author for permission should be addressed to the following email: Theauthor2004@gmail.com

Limitation of Liability/Disclaimer of Warranty: The publisher and the author make no representations or warranties on the accuracy or completeness of the contents of this work and specifically disclaim all warranties, including without limitation warranties of fitness for particular purpose. No warranty may be created or extended by sales representatives, promoters, or written sales materials. The advice and strategies contained herein may not be suitable for every situation. This work is sold with the understanding that the publisher or the author is not engaged in rendering legal, accounting, or other professional services. If professional assistance is required, the services of a competent professional person should be sought. Neither the publisher nor the author shall be liable for damages arising therefrom. The fact that an organization or website is referred to in this work as a citation and a potential source of further information does not mean that the author or the publisher endorses the information the organization or website may provide or recommendations it may make. Further, readers should be aware that Internet Websites listed in this work may have changed or disappeared between when this work was written and when it is read.

Ordering Information:
Bookstores, wholesalers, corporations, associations, and others.

Please email enquiries to:
Theauthor2004@gmail.com

DEDICATION

To my mom Natacshia Richards my biggest cheerleader. She is always pushing me even when I didn't feel like pushing myself. To my guardian angel, my Dad Tracy, God had bigger plans for you. Please continue to watch over us all. I Love and miss you so much. To my Stepdad Bo thanks for stepping up and loving us. To my entire village. There are so many of you. You all have stood by my side through it all. You encourage me, You inspire me and when I fall you're right there making sure I get up. To all my readers and those who do not know me, let me pass on to you what my mother gave me. You are not here to be mediocre and you are Limitless Potential. Go out there and show the world what you're made of.

INTRODUCTION

Have you been to your first job interview yet? Chances are you will go on many interviews throughout your lifetime. Hi, my name is Tracie-Ann Joy Richards, I am a 17 years old senior at Clara Barton High School. I recently went to my very first job interview. Although my mom prepared me for it, I did not get the job due to me not having enough experience. They chose the best candidate for the job. Yes, I was a little disappointed. I'm sure this will not be my last so I brushed it off as a lesson. Denzel Washington had over 15 auditions before he was chosen for a part. Going on an interview can be scary, especially when it's your first. You really don't know what to expect. Before you go on an interview, research the company you want to work for. They may research you as well by looking into your social media pages and links you connect to them. Do you know the job description? If your answer is no, why not? You want to research that as well. You need to make sure you're capable of completing the work and you also want to see if it's something you want to do. You don't want to go on an interview and find out information you could have just read on the company's website. They will be very impressed if you walked into your interview knowing their mission statement and the name of the CEO. I wrote this book because like me, I'm sure so many young and some older people have no clue about what they should be doing prior to their job interview. Some people were never taught how to conduct themselves, what to say and always ask questions at the end. Take notes so you can set up your questions for later and see if what you were told is Qsomething you can work with. My book will teach the basics. How to speak and what to say as you enter the building. How you should greet your interviewer and own the room as you walk into it. While walking with full confidence. You want to make sure everything about you speaks to the Best Candidate for the position. My book will also have you digging deep inside yourself to learn more about you. Things like your strengths and weaknesses and how you can turn your weakness into something positive. Not everyone will get the job and if you have that kind of resilience no one is going to stop me, you will never quit being the best version of yourself. It is normal to feel disappointed when you worked hard for something and did not get it. Don't allow not getting the job define you. Confront it and go over your interview questions and answers and what you've learned from that job interview. You can then make changes if need be with your approach, your answers, greetings etc. This way you're prepared for the next one. What does success really mean to you? What will people really remember you for? The reason for going over what you've learned is so you can continue making yourself great. What's for you will always be for you. So if you did not get the opposition just know a better one is in store for you.

Get your journal out. Let me take this journey with you. I'm ready if you are. You have nothing to lose.

"Victory Is Always Possible For The Person Who Refuses To Stop Fighting"

-UNKNOWN-

* * * * *

"Success Isnt About How Much Money You Make; It's About The Difference You Make In People's Lives"

- MICHELLE OBAMA-

Table of Contents

Chapter One: Research The Company 1

Chapter Two: Prepare A Resume And Cover Letter 4

Chapter Three: Examine The Job Description 12

Chapter Four: Why Do You Want To Work Here............. 14

Chapter Five: Tell Me About Yourself................... 18

Chapter Six: How To Introduce Yourself........................ 21

Chapter Seven: What Are Your Strengths And Weakness.. 23

Chapter Eight: Take Notes And Ask Questions 27

Chapter Nine: Dressing Appropriately 30

Chapter Ten: Sending That Thank You Email................... 32

About The Author 35

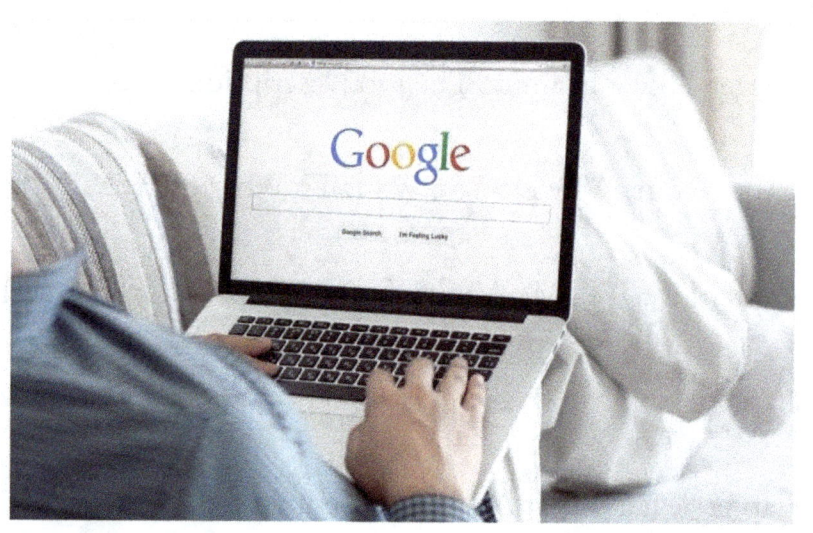

Chapter One

RESEARCH THE COMPANY

Researching the company you're applying for is very important when preparing for your job interview. You can also do your research before applying for the job. When preparing for your interview it allows you to know who you're really going to be working for when you get the position. I used the word WHEN to speak about getting the position in the universe. Say it yourself. WHEN I GET THE POSITION. Your research will also assist you when you have to answer questions. You already know what the company is looking for. Do they have a mission statement?

Such as, America Runs On Dunkin- Dunkin Donuts, I'm Loving It - Mcdonalds or even They're GRRREAT - Frosted Flakes. Learn it so you have to recite it during your interview. A slogan is a way the company likes to get everyone's attention and your way of letting them know that they have yours. A slogan is also a short reminder of the value a brand offers their customers. Why not allow them to know you're already ahead of the game and ready to be onboard. All of the research increases your comfort level. You don't want to walk in there not knowing much about the company. You also want to do your research to see if it's a great fit for you as well. You don't want to find out you have to work for a company where you have to work on religious observance days. Do your homework.

A FEW QUESTIONS TO ANSWER WHILE DOING YOUR RESEARCH

1. HOW LONG HAS THE COMPANY BEEN IN BUSINESS
2. WHO IS THE CEO
3. WHAT YEAR WAS IT FOUNDED
4. WHAT'S THE SLOGAN OR MISSION STATEMENT
5. ARE THEY FLEXIBLE WITH WORK HOURS AND VACATION SCHEDULES
6. WHAT IS THE DRESS CODE
7. CAN WE HAVE LONG HAIR
8. DO THEY OFFER TRAINING

Chapter Two

PREPARE A RESUME AND COVER LETTER

Just because you didn't have experience doesn't mean you can't write a convincing resume. You will write down all of your accomplishments, training, awards, volunteering services. Make sure your skills are also down. You can add cpr training, girl scouts leader, dance captain, football captain. Chess champs, spelling bee winner. You can add volunteers at school to tutor, office aid. Make sure you add that you volunteered to read to the elderly in the nursing home or went grocery shopping or doing the laundry for your grandparents, friends or a stranger, and babysitting. You're showing the interviewer you have empathy, integrity, your kind hearted and your a team player to name a few.

Adding a cover letter will offer more relevant information about your qualifications in relation to the position you're applying for. If written currently you can stand out from all the rest. You will explain why you're interested. It allows you to tell your story before being interviewed.

Also you want to monitor your social media so many employers today check applicant social media pages. They want to see what you are showing the world publicity about yourself. They use this to see if you're a perfect candidate for their establishment. So be very mindful about what you're posting before going for a job. I knew we were all young and we started these social media pages a few years ago. It's time to clean them up - delete what needs to be deleted off o your page or delete it and start a new one. You will definitely know what needs to be done after reviewing for page and the links you have attached to it.

NAME
ADDRESS
CELL/PHONE NUMBER

February 24, 2020

Brooklyn DDSO-Human Resources Office
888 Fountain Avenue
Brooklyn, NY 11239

To whom it may concern;

I am responding to your postings EOA #20-27 for Developmental Assistant 3. I am currently working in this title.

Attached you will find my resume and noted 20 plus years of experience with OPWDD. I believe I possess the necessary skills to be effective as a DA3 having previously served and worked at Shirtz 1, with all aspects of the team. I am looking forward to interviewing for this title and position.

Sincerely,

NAME

Name

Address

Cell or Phone Number

EMAIL

OBJECTIVE:
TO OBTAIN A POSITION TO UTILIZE MY PRESENT SKILLS AND FURTHER MY CAREER

EXPERIENCE:
JUNE. 2019 - PRESENT: BROOKLYN DEVELOPMENTAL CENTER, 888 FOUNTAIN AVE, BKLYN, NY 11208

DEVELOPMENTAL ASSISTANT 3
Supervised DA1, DA2, Direct Support Professional staff in carrying out the day to day aspects of individuals residing in OPWDD's Developmental Center, Shirtz 1 ICF and IRA's Cozine, Cleveland and Hawthorne. Responsibilities include: Staffing Schedules, ACUMATICA, SLMS Monitoring, Class Trainings, Inservice Trainings, Service Plan Meetings, TIMES and Facility Max updates, Conducting and Monitoring Fire Drills Etc.

DEC. 2018 – JUNE 2019

DEVELOPMENTAL ASSISTANT 2–

Supervised DA1, Direct Support Professional staff in carrying out the day to day aspects of individuals residing in OPWDD's Shirtz ICF Responsibilities included ACUMATICA, SLMS monitoring, Class Trainings, Inservice Trainings, Service Plan Meetings, TIMES and Facility Max updates, Staffing schedules, overtime Management, Fire Drills etc.

JUNE 2004- DEC 2018

DEVELOPMENTAL ASSISTANT 1

Worked on the grounds of Brooklyn Developmental Center in Building 3 the medically frail unit and in Community IRA's Voorhies and 53rd Street Residence, supervising staff, making schedules, monitoring overtime, maintaining a safe work environment, shopping and the staff schedule, purchasing for the individuals, ensuring goals are met.

AUG 1996 – JUNE 2004

DIRECT SUPPORT PROFESSIONAL

Worked hands on in the community at 64th street residence and Day Program with individuals. Grocery and clothes shopping for individuals, community inclusion trips, medical appointments etc.

EDUCATION:

2005-2007-Healthcare Administration Course of Study Completed, Master of Science – Almeda University

Name
Address
Email
Cell Phone

OBJECTIVE: TO OBTAIN A POSITION TO UTILIZE MY PRESENT SKILLS AND FURTHER MY CAREER

WORK EXPERIENCE:
List work experience in chronological order

Example
(Years From - To)   (Location)
JUNE 2021-PRESENT BROOKLYN DDSO, Brooklyn, NY
(Title)
DEVELOPMENTAL ASST 1 – Kingsland IRA
(List description and job duties/responsibilities)
Shift Supervisor with a staff of five. Responsibilities are adequate staffing numbers for each shift. Active Treatment for the individuals, medical appts, shopping. Monitoring EHR, SLMS and Times for staff. Conducting Fire Drills, maintaining a clean, safe work environment. Holding and attending meetings, giving staff in services when necessary.

EDUCATIONAL BACKGROUND

Graduate of (High School Name)

ACADEMIC ACHIEVEMENTS - (List if any)

ACADEMIC PROGRAMS – (List if any)

PROFESSIONAL SUMMARY – (List if any)

SKILLS & PROFICIENCIES – (List if any)

VOLUNTEER WORK – (List if any)

Tracie -Ann J. Richards

SAMPLE

WORK EXPERIENCE

Babysitter (Richards Family) 2014-2021
Planned and implemented activities based on children's developmental milestones
- Monitored children while their parents were away
- Met children's nutritional needs by preparing nutritious snacks
- Supervised hygiene by changing diapers and assisting in washing hands and bathing
- Taught social skills to ensure social acceptability
- Assessed children's developmental needs and met them appropriately
- Discussed progress and limitations with parents when necessary

EDUCATIONAL BACKGROUND

Clara Barton High School for Health Professions, Brooklyn NY- Class of 2022 GPA: 92.62

ACADEMIC ACHIEVEMENTS:
- Perfect Attendance Award (Spring 2019)
- High Honor Roll (Fall 2019, Spring 2020, Fall 2020)
- Perfect Attendance (Fall 2020)
- High Honor Roll (Fall 2020-2021)
- High Honor Roll (Spring 2020-2021)

ACADEMIC PROGRAMS:
PARTICIPANT: Clara Barton Gateway Program
PARTICIPANT: College Now
- Attending college-level courses at Clara Barton High School
- Worked on skills to become college-ready
PARTICIPANT: Medical Assistant Program

PROFESSIONAL SUMMARY

I am currently a High School student at Clara Barton High School, willing to learn new skills. I am dedicated to finishing what I have started as well. I am also a multi-tasker, I work very well with others, and I am considerate with everyone I encounter.

SKILLS & PROFICIENCIES
- Proficient in Teamwork
- Copywriting and copy editing
- Proficient in Communucation
- Proficient in dedication
- Proficient in Time Mangement

VOLUNTEER WORK

Girl Scout-Breast Cancer Walk
Girl Scout-Cleaning up prospect Park
2014-2016

Chapter Three

EXAMINE THE JOB DESCRIPTION

Carefully examining the job description not only will it impress the interviewer because you paid attention to their details. It can help you be more knowledgeable about the job you're going for. The description is a list of qualifications the employer is looking for in a candidate. This helps you to position yourself as the best candidate when knowing what they're looking for. Read the employees about the page also to gain more information about their key players. Turn the descriptions into questions. Example is the job description you must be able to work with a team. Turn it into a question: ask yourself when was the last time you worked with a team and how did you handle challenges you've overcome while you worked with them.

You can answer by saying I worked with the football team and during this time me and another player kept going up for the same position. The coach allowed us both to try out for it and the most qualified one was given the position to head the team.

<u>OR</u>

I had a project in class and one of the students was not pulling her weight. Instead of telling the teacher we spoke to me and the other team mates spoke to her to see what was the problem. She explained she was having a situation at home that was holding her back. We all decided to work with her together during the hours she did not have to care for her sick grandmother.

So by going through the description once again is a powerful tool to prepare you before walking into the room. Some employees will make up questions according to the job description.

Chapter Four

WHY DO YOU WANT TO WORK HERE

Answer the question of Why do you want to work here?

_____
_____
_____
_____
_____
_____

The best way to prepare for this question is if you once again read up on the description of the position. Research the company and learn about the company's mission. Explain to the interview what appealed to you the most.

EXAMPLE

I'd love the opportunity to work with a company that won't need to make a difference in others' lives. I see this as a way for me to join your team and add my contributions and deliver exceptional results to the company. It allows me to learn more about myself and develop more skills through your training program. This question may seem simple but it can determine the final outcome of your interview. You will be able to have a chance to convince the interviewer to hire you. It will also show how credible you are -

- » Sound Enthusiastic
- » Make sure you show how you want to align yourself with their mission
- » Show that you've done your research you want to show Authenticity
- » Avoid answers such as

"I want to grow with your company"

"I feel i',m the best candidate"

THING TO AVOID SAYING

1. Sorry I'm late - You should never be late for an interview- On time is late and early is on time is what my mother says.
2. Please don't say you're nervous- Although it's natural to be nervous and try not to look at it. If you had to describe your feelings use words like excited, overjoyed. This sends a letter message to the interviewer.
3. Avoid talking bad about your previous employer if you had one. It doesn't set a ground tone. Remember those who talk bad about others may talk about you as well. You don't want your potential employer to think you will do the same to them.
4. Avoid telling the employee you see yourself taking their job in a few years. It's great to be confident but it come across a little bullyish
5. Avoid telling the interview all of the problems you may be having at home. This may have them wondering if you can handle the job.
6. Never use the words I don't know. You can say I don't have that information right now but can get back to them later on.

Chapter Five

TELL ME ABOUT YOURSELF

Practice your answers for common asked questions - Tell me a little bit about yourself

Here are a few tips when answering this question you want to introduce yourself once again and let them know you are thankful for the opportunity to interview for this position. If you haven't handed them your resume this is the best for me to do so. You want to smile and posture up. Don't slouch in the chair and look everywhere around the room other than the interviewer when speaking to them. You want to make eye contact. It's ok if you wrote down some key points to remember to discuss, just don't keep your head down on your paper the entire time. You want to smile and speak up. You don't want the interviewer asking you to respect yourself because you're speaking very poorly. They should not be struggling to hear what you are saying. Being prepared ahead of time can calm your nerves. Practice answering this question before your interview and present yourself as knowledgeable and confident. This shows your potential employers you're the right fit for the position. Get personal but not too personal. I am the great granddaughter of a Reverend. I am the middle child with siblings that can get on my very last nerves (laugh). You're trying to break the ice in the room with a little humor. The interviewer may laugh too. This part of your interview should be the easiest for you because you're talking about yourself. You don't need to practice that, you know yourself better than anyone else. Let the interviewer know you are very dedicated and disciplined in everything that you do. That you also work hard towards your goals and don't stop until you complete it. You can also add I was previously girl scout leader, football captain or even a dance captain. These all sharpened my leadership skills in learning how to be a team player, problem solver and good communicator. I get along with others and am not afraid to ask questions. I am very punctual. A wise lady (My Mom) once said early is on time and on time is late. Don't do too much talking. You don't have to tell your entire life story just enough info you think they would need to get the job. The most impactful information. This will make you a great candidate.

Chapter Six

HOW TO INTRODUCE YOURSELF

When you arrive you want to greet the person at the desk with a hello. My name is Jane Doe and I'm here for a 10am interview for the manager's position. Not everyone iis pleasant. Make sure you are humble, patient and kind. The interviewer may ask the person you greeted how your attitude was and were you pleasant. Finally you enter the room, you are to walk in like you own the room. You greet everyone with a smile. Introduce yourself with your full name. You keep your head held high with so much confidence as if you already landed this interview. Body language says it all. Your body language can speak before you open your mouth. You don't want to walk with your head held down. That can read you have low self esteem. Whether it's one interviewer or more when they introduce themselves, write their name down. This way you can remember their names. Remember first impressions can play a major role in how the interviewer sees you as a candidate for the position. You want to show them you are professional and can conduct yourself as such. Practice with someone at home before the actual interview.

Chapter Seven

WHAT ARE YOUR STRENGTHS AND WEAKNESS

Although you may have many strengths when answering this question you want to use the strengths that identify with the job description. They ask this question to see if you aligned with what they're looking for and needed for the position. They want to make sure you're the perfect candidate and a great asset to the establishment. Remember they're building a team of excellence. Now is your chance to brag a little bit about yourself in the most humble way. Without sounding conceited. You can break your strengths down when listing them, those you feel that make you the most unique should be at the top of your list as well. For example, I am humble, kind, and always on time. Strengths obtained through work or school such as filing or communication skills or through Education such as filing , computer specialist. You can also mention your degrees or certificates. Narrow it down to at least 4-5 strengths. The ones you feel are easy to talk about the most. You may not need them all,It's just great to have more than less. Strengths such as a Team Player, A Problem Solver. An example of what you can say, I am a great communicator and I work well with others. I know you may not want to discuss what you're not good at. Think of a weakness you can or have turned into something positive. When asked, always begin with your strengths. You don't want to put a negative in front of a positive. Everyone has a weakness so don't get scared about this question. Not everyone is prepared to answer this question. This chapter is preparing youtube to be comfortable when answering this question. Examples of weaknesses can be Being too hard on yourself, Always trying to please everyone, micro managing an deven disliking saying no. When picking a weakness, always come up with one you have a solution to. Don't get nervous, this is why you practice at home first. Practice makes perfect or as I see it practice makes it closer to perfection. You will be more prepared when practicing at home. You can also practice when you don't have an interview just to have things packed. The interviewer's goal in asking what your weaknesses are is so they can see how you overcome challenges. What you need to do is think back at your past experiences where you were faced with a task or situation you had to find a solution for. The end results should be what you've learned from it. Here is an example.

Weakness -I like to help everyone and don't like saying no. I find myself taking on more than I can handle with so many deadlines.

Turned the weakness into a strength - I learned how to say no or not right now. This way I can manage my time much better when taking on tasks and not burn myself out by trying to meet so many deadlines all at once. My time management skills have gotten much better. I also let others know that in order for me to give them my best, they have to give me some time to finish what I've already started. I Don't like being late with my work. To tell you the truth I like my work to be finished before the deadline. This gives me time to breathe before my next task.

LIST OF STRENGTHS

1. Team player
2. A problem solving
3. Humble
4. Kind
5. Punctual
6. People person
7. Enthusiasm
8. Patience
9. Trustworthy
10. Respectful
11. Flexibility
12. Creativity
13. Originality
14. Goal Digger
15. Empathy
16. Leadership
17. Fast learner
18. Positive mindset
19. Organizational skills
20. Strong work ethics

Chapter Eight

TAKE NOTES AND ASK QUESTIONS

Don't worry, it's appropriate to take notes during your interview. You can refer to these notes at the end when the interviewer asks if you have any questions. Always remember the way you answer the interviewer's questions can either get you the job or disqualify you from getting it. It's not alway having the experience that can get you hired. With so much going on it's easy to forget some of the highlights of the interview. This is why it's very important you want to take your notes. Your note taking is showing the interviewer your paying attention and don't want to forget anything. Now, those who can not really multitask, i don't want you to miss out on very important information by trying to keep up and do both. You don't want to look confused while doing so as well. What you should do is pay close attention to what the interviewer is saying. Your note taking can also assist you with figuring out if this is the best job for you. It will also assist you with writing your interviewer a thank you email. You should send it out that evening or the following morning. I will speak about this in the next few chapters.

Here are a few questions you can ask when asked if you have any questions.

1. What is your favorite part of working for this company?
2. What is a typical day like at this company for the position?
3. What is the next step in the job process?
4. What would be my daily responsibilities?
5. What is your definition of leadership?
6. Who will I be working closely with?
7. Is there any growth for me in this company?
8. Does the company offer training?
9. What characteristics do I need to succeed in this position?
9. How would my performance be measured in this position?

Chapter Nine

DRESSING APPROPRIATELY

Whether it's your first 2nd or even third job interview you must always dress to impress. I will say this again if I haven't said it already. You must make a lasting impression. Appearance can make a major impact when meeting someone for the first time. Your hygiene must be neat and clean. It doesn't matter whether it's the janitor position or manager's position, you want to walk into that company dressed as if you're going for the highest paid position. You dress as you want to be seen representing the company, the easy they would want to be represented.

Prepare your clothes from the night before. What you wear is a part of who you are. Here are some ideas for your attire. Females can wear a pants suit and a blouse, A blazer blouse and a skirt or pants. She can also wear a dress. The dress or skirt should not be mini. Nice clean shoes flats or heels. Men can wear a suit or slacks and a button down shirt with a tie. Make sure your shoes are clean. No sneakers or caps. No one should have loud colored hair and your nails should not be long that it reaches the door before you do. Remember, nothing too short or tight. Spit your gum out before entering the room and chew up the mint. You do not want to be speaking with anything in your mouth. Nothing lacy or sheer. No muscle shirts or belly tops. Try not to wear too much perfume. You want your confidence alone to take over the room, not your smell. It's better to be too dressed up than not too casual. You're more likely to be taken seriously if you're dressed up professionally. Turn back, Remember to take out that gum.

Chapter Ten

SENDING THAT THANK YOU EMAIL

Those who are really interested in the position should send the interviewer a thank you email. Send you an email the night of or day after your interview. The notes I discussed in the previous chapter will now help you draft up your email. It will definitely come in handy. All of the highlights you've written down will now allow the interviewer to see how much you paid attention. When sending an email you're reminding the interviewer of your skills and qualities.

Now is your last chance to include anything you forgot to say you feel is important that they know. Make sure you mention your skills you possess in the job description. Highlights and any additional information they've included during your interview such as punctuality and names of any team players. Restate why you want the position again. It's like a reinforcement. Let the interviewer know how you will make a significant contribution to the company.

HERE IS AN EXAMPLE EMAIL

Make sure to include your name and position you interviewed for in the subject line. You're doing this to ensure your email is opened and read. Here is an example.

Hello (Your interviewer name) It was my pleasure meeting you and speaking to you yesterday. I've learned so much more about the company and position. Thank you for the opportunity, our conversation made me want the position even more and Ican see myself working for this establishment. (You can add in a reason why by using the notes you'd taken down during your interview) I was excited to hear the company trains you in different areas and that there is growth in the company for me. I was also excited to know that after three years the company will give you a stipend if you want to return back to school. Because I feed the homeless every year it really interests me to work for a company who gives back and feeds the homeless and has coat drives. I am not concerned at all about what characteristics I need to succeed in the company because I possess them as well. I'm sure my skills as a fast learner will get me where I need to be in the company with the thing sI do not know as yet. If you need any further information please feel free to contact me. I am looking forward to hearing from you soon. Thank you for your time.

Sincerely

(Your First and Last Name)

I am not saying that this email is definitely going to seal the deal and get you the position. I will say you will be remembered for it while making their decision.

ABOUT THE AUTHOR

Tracie-Ann Joy Richards is a 17 year old senior attending Clara Barton High School in Brooklyn Ny. Coming from a background of Guyanese and Trinadadian descent. Who parents instilled morals and values that taught her the importance of hard work, good work ethics and to never settle for mediocrity. Growing up education was enforced in her household in addition to exploration. Tracie-Ann will be attending college this fall. Tracie-Ann is a young entrepreneur who started her online boutique accessories business in 2019 called Glam Accessories. Tracie has traveled the world since she was a young girl. She has been to places like London England,

Bahamas, Puerto Rico, Dominican Republic, Mexico, Jamaica and Trinidad. An Honor roll student, CPR certified, Girl Scouts Leader Tracie-Ann doesn't mind giving back to the community. Tracie-Ann has been involved in coat drives, toy drives and feeding the homeless. Tracie recently enrolled in the Dorot Program where they form friendships with the elderly by creating bonds and providing assistance by reading to them, having a conversation or just sending them a card. It is her desire to always have an open mindset, put God first and walk in her purpose. She will maintain a standard of excellence and to do so with integrity.

www.ingramcontent.com/pod-product-compliance
Lightning Source LLC
Chambersburg PA
CBHW071846290426
44109CB00017B/1939